YORK PERSONAL TUTORS

Poetry

Paul Pascoe

Longman

York Press

YORK PRESS
322 Old Brompton Road, London SW5 9JH

PEARSON EDUCATION LIMITED
Edinburgh Gate, Harlow
Essex CM20 2JE, United Kingdom
Associated companies, branches and representatives throughout
the world

© Librairie du Liban *Publishers* and Pearson Education Limited
2000

First published 2000

ISBN 0582 40424-X

Designed by Shireen Nathoo Design, London
Illustrated by Spike Gerrell, Mike Perkins, Sholto Walker
Photographs: p.11 Sporting Pictures (UK) Ltd.; p.21 Rex Features;
p.29 Mary Evans Picture Library; p.33 NHPA; p.38 Science Photo
Library; p.59 Tony Stone Images / Christopher Thomas; p.72
Heather Angel; p.74 Images Colour Library; p.89 Rex Features.

*The author and publishers wish to thank the following for permission
to use copyright material:*

Carcanet Press Ltd for William Carlos Williams, 'The Loving
Dexterity' from *Collected Poems 1939-1962*, Vol. II. Copyright ©
1962 by William Carlos Williams; Curtis Brown (Aust) on behalf of
the author for A D Hope, 'The Bed' from *Collected Poems*, Angus
and Robertson; Andre Deutsch Ltd for Ogden Nash, 'The Pizza'
from *Verses From 1929 On* by Ogden Nash. Copyright © 1957 by
Ogden Nash, renewed © 1985 by Frances Nash, Isabel Nash
Eberstadt and Linnell Nash Smith; and Ogden Nash, 'The Ant'
from *Verses From 1929 On* by Ogden Nash, first appeared in *The
Saturday Evening Post*. Copyright © 1935 by Ogden Nash; Faber and
Faber Ltd for extracts from Wendy Cope, 'Strugnell's Haiku' and
'From June to December' from *Making Cocoa for Kingsley Amis* by
Wendy Cope; Wendy Cope, 'A Green Song' and an extract from
'Kindness to Animals' from *Serious Concerns* by Wendy Cope;
extracts from T S Eliot, 'Burbank with a Baedeker' and 'The Waste
Land' from *Collected Poems 1909-1962* by T S Eliot; Philip Larkin,
'Water' from *Collected Poems*. Copyright © 1988, 1989 by the Estate
of Philip Larkin; an extract from Thom Gunn, 'Considering the
Snail' from *Collected Poems* by Thom Gunn. Copyright © 1994 by
Thom Gunn; extracts from W H Auden, 'In Memory of W B Yeats'
from W H Auden: *Collected Poems* by W H Auden, ed. Edward
Mendelson. Copyright © 1940 and renewed 1968 by W H Auden,
and W H Auden, 'Night Mail from *W H Auden: Collected Poems* by
W H Auden, ed. Edward Mendelson. Copyright © 1938, renewed
1966 by W H Auden; Harvard University Press and the Trustees of
Amherst College for Emily Dickinson, 'Poem 445' from *The Poems
of Emily Dickinson*, ed. Ralph W Franklin, The Belknap Press of
Harvard University Press. Copyright © 1951, 1955, 1979 by the
President and Fellows of Harvard College, copyright © 1998 by the
President and Fellows of Harvard College; David Higham Associates
on behalf of the Estate of the author for Herbert Read, 'The Happy
Warrior' from *The Scene of War*, Sinclair Stevenson; International
Music Publications Ltd for an extract from 'You're the Top', words
and music by Cole Porter, Warner Chappell Music Ltd. Copyright
©1934 Harms Inc; Evan Jones for 'The Lament of the Banana Man'
included in *The Penguin Book of Caribbean Verse in English* (1986);
Richard Kenney for 'Plume' from *Orrery* by Richard Kenney,
Atheneum (1985); Barbara Levy Literary Agency on behalf of
George Sassoon for extracts from Siegfried Sassoon, 'At the
Cenotaph' from *Collected Poems of Siegfried Sassoon* by Siegfried
Sassoon. Copyright © 1918, 1920 by E P Dutton. Copyright © 1936,
1946, 1947, 1948 by Siegfried Sassoon, and 'Does it Matter' from
Collected Poems of Siegfried Sassoon by Siegfried Sassoon. Copyright
© 1918 by E P Dutton, renewed1946 by Siegfried Sassoon; The
Marvell Press for Philip Larkin, 'At Grass' from *The Less Deceived*;
Music Sales Ltd for an extract from 'Yesterday', words and music by
John Lennon and Paul McCartney. Copyright ©1965 Northern
Songs, all rights reserved; Laurence Pollinger Ltd on behalf of the
author for extracts from Denise Levertov, 'The Dead Butterfly' from
Collected Earlier Poems 1940-1960 by Denise Levertov. Copyright ©
1948, 1979 by Denise Levertov, and Denise Levertov, 'The Secret'
from *Poems 1960-1967* by Denise Levertov. Copyright © 1964 by
Denise Levertov; Random House UK for an extract from Robert
Frost, 'Stopping by Woods on a Snowy Evening' from *The Poetry of
Robert Frost*, ed, Edward Connery Lathem, Jonathan Cape; Rogers
Coleridge and White Ltd on behalf of the author for an extract from
Brian Patten, 'Where Are You Now Batman?' from *Grinning Jack* by
Brian Patten, Unwin Paperbacks (1990). Copyright © Brian Patten,
1990; Vernon Scannell for 'Jailbird' and 'View from a Deckchair';
Watson, Little Ltd on behalf of the author for an extract from D J
Enright, 'Blue Umbrellas' from *Bread Rather Than Blossoms* by D J
Enright, Carcanet (1968); A P Watt Ltd on behalf of Michael B Yeats
for W B Yeats, 'The Arrow'

Every effort has been made to trace the copyright holders but if any
have been inadvertently overlooked the publishers will be pleased to
make the necessary arrangement at the first opportunity.

Typeset by Gem Graphics, Trenance, Mawgan Porth, Cornwall
Colour reproduction and film output by Spectrum Colour
Printed in Malaysia, VVP

CONTENTS

INTRODUCTION

The National Curriculum
About this book

For GCSE you are required to read a range of poetry of different types and from different periods and traditions. You will also be expected to show that you can grasp meanings beyond the literal and engage with ideas, themes and language.

This guide **does not** attempt to provide comprehensive coverage of all aspects of the poetry curriculum. It does attempt to set you thinking about various key aspects of poetry by looking at specific examples.

It is assumed, probably unfairly, that you are new to poetry and may not even like it much. This guide tries to anticipate some of the difficulties and suggest ways in which they might be tackled. It is divided into sections:

- **Aliens among us** explores how our ordinary, down-to-earth, everyday world employs many 'poetic' techniques that may seem alien to those who dislike poetry. We see that even the least poetically inclined of us already possesses the basic means of travel to the planet Poetry.

- **Variety is the spice of life** tries to dispel the notion that poetry is concerned only with 'soft' and 'romantic' subjects. Any field of human experience, including science, may be the object of a poet's attention.

- **What's it all about?** looks more closely at what poems really mean and considers what some people often refer to as 'hidden meaning'.

- **Weird and wonderful words** moves from pure subject-matter and takes a look at how poets use words.

- **All that technical stuff** looks at the sound of poetry and at some of the bewildering terminology associated with this subject. It examines the role of rhythm, rhyme and the use of line divisions.

- **Putting it all together** attempts to draw the threads together and examine some poems from a number of points of view. There is advice on how to approach texts but the commentaries in this section should not be regarded as model answers.

GCSE syllabuses refer to pre-twentieth-century and multicultural texts. In this book poetry has been treated as a seamless activity. Nevertheless, within the space available, there is a cross-section of poems from different periods and cultures.

DID YOU KNOW?

There is now a National Poetry Day. In 1995, there was a vote held for 'the nation's favourite poem'. It was won by the poem *If* by Rudyard Kipling (1865–1936), which starts:

If you can keep your head when all about you
Are losing theirs and blaming it on you...

ALIENS AMONG US –
POETRY IN EVERDAY LIFE

Words and meaning

Getting the 'joke'

The effect of words

This section shows that, in some ways at least, poetry is simply a special version of what is familiar to us all. If we think more closely about how we use language in our everyday lives, we may be better able to understand the workings of poetry.

Words, words, words

It may be blindingly obvious but students often forget that their most direct connection with poetry is language itself Sometimes poetry may seem to be written in an obscure code and it is all too easy to overlook that we all use and respond to language in extraordinarily complex ways

DID YOU KNOW?

Words can do so many things. *The Shorter Oxford English Dictionary* has no fewer than six pages of entries covering that simplest of words, 'let'. How many uses of the word can you think of?

Take a simple word like 'run'. What does it mean? 'To move with quick steps', seems a reasonable enough answer at first but run your eye over this list:

- My mother ran up a set of curtains on the sewing machine.

- John ran up an enormous debt.

- The motorist ran down the stray dog then ran over a stray cat!

- The accountant ran over some figures with his client.

- Jane now runs the business because her husband has decided to run for election.

- I've run out of examples!

Not much moving with quick steps there, but we have no difficulty in responding to the shifting meanings because we are familiar with the language. As we shall see, poems often require you to do something similar but in new and unfamiliar ways. For the moment here is a simple example. The basic sense is clear but what extra meaning can you extract by considering the different possible senses of some of the words? Think about the comparisons between the prisoner (jailbird) and a real bird.

Jailbird

His plumage is dun,
Talons long but blunt.
His appetite is indiscriminate.
He has no mate and sleeps alone
In a high nest built of brick and steel.
He sings at night
A long song, sad and silent.
He cannot fly.

(Vernon Scannell, 1922–)

The naming of parts

Poets also use words, not just for their plain meaning, but for the effect they have on our feelings and emotions. For some people, this is what they dislike about poetry; they may think using words in this way as 'soft' or 'woolly'.

We may not be as hard-headed as we think. Technology may seem to inhabit a different universe from poetry, yet we give names to chemical products, machinery and electronic equipment that are decidedly more poetic than scientific.

The potions and lotions that we apply to ourselves all have chemical functions but it's doubtful that many people would prefer to regard their shampoo, for instance, as a mere detergent! A quick glance through the colour supplements will uncover product names such as:

Eternity
Mimosa pour Moi
primordiale nuit
Foamburst Gel
even *Poeme!*

Ah, that wonderful smell of Cyclomethicone, aluminium zirconium tetrachlorohydrex...

THINK ABOUT IT

Why are so many of these products given a French-sounding name?

Only connect

Question: *Why did the traffic light turn red?*
Answer: *Wouldn't you if you had to change in the middle of the street?*

You may find that an awful joke or uproariously funny but to make sense of it at all, those simple words need to trigger some quite intricate thought processes. You need to understand *context* – where you find traffic lights and what they do – and you need to appreciate play on the *literal* meaning of red and its *metaphorical* associations with embarrassment. We need to make connections in order to 'explain' the joke to ourselves.

A lot of poetry depends on our brains working in similar ways, so that we can see the 'joke', as it were.

THINK ABOUT IT

Strange as it may seem, even the simplest of jokes often depend on sensitivity to context, wordplay, ambiguity (double meanings or uncertain meanings), and allusion (unexplained reference), something you certainly need when reading poetry.

Question: *Which vegetables did Noah refuse to take on board the Ark?*
Answer: *Leeks!*

You need to appreciate wordplay — the double meaning of leek/leak — but you also need to appreciate the *allusion,* or unexplained reference, to Noah and the Ark, otherwise the joke makes no sense at all. Poetry is full of allusions.

N
O
T
E
S

You need your wits about you to explain these lines by the seventeenth-century poet, John Donne (1572-1631):

Twice or thrice had I loved thee,
Before I knew thy face or name;

(From **Aire and Angels**, 1592)

How is it possible to love someone before you have even met? There's a kind of joke in there somewhere.

Names

What's in a name? that which we call a rose
By any other name would smell as sweet.

From **Romeo and Juliet** (1595) by William Shakespeare

Perhaps, actually names are rather important to us. Some parents go through agonies mulling over possible names for their child.

Personal names don't actually mean anything any more, even if they once did. You may be called Butcher or Baker (probably not Candlestick Maker) but it would be pure coincidence if those names denoted your family trade. Yet we respond quite powerfully to names for no obvious reason. Sue is simply a contraction of Susan, yet creates quite a different image in our minds.

DID YOU KNOW?
The actor John Wayne (1907-1979), who was famous for his roles in Westerns, was really called Marion Michael Morrison. Do you think he'd have been such a successful film star if he'd kept his real name?

NOTES

As we shall see, poetry asks us to respond to words (which do have dictionary meanings as well) rather in the way we so readily react to names.

Finally, to return to where we began. Poets say things in strange ways, don't they? No more strange perhaps than the remarks of football star, would-be actor, philosopher and poet, Eric Cantona:

'When the seagulls follow the trawler it is because they think sardines will be thrown into the sea.'

Whatever he may have meant, the fact that he expressed himself in imagery rather than factual language seems to have made much more of an impression than if he had used 'plain' English.

KEY CONCEPTS

We use and respond to some of the methods of poetry even if we never read any ✳

You should use this awareness to build an understanding of poetry itself ✳

Poetry draws on the meaning and the connotation of words ✳

HIGHER PERFORMANCE

In this extract from a poem by John Keats (1795–1821) an ardent lover, Porphyro, lays out a selection of rare foods to beguile his beloved Madeline:

And still she slept an azure-lidded sleep,
In blanched linen, smooth, and lavender'd,
While he from forth the closet brought a heap
Of candied apple, quince, and plum, and gourd;
With jellies soother than the creamy curd,
And lucent syrops, tinct with
Manna and dates, in argosy transferr'd
From Fez; and spiced dainties, every one,
From silken Samarcand to cedar'd Lebanon.

These delicates he heap'd with glowing hand
On golden dishes and in baskets bright
Of wreathed silver: sumptuous they stand
In the retired quiet of the night,
Filling the chilly room with perfume light.

(from **The Eve of St Agnes**, 1819)

The modern restaurateur also tries to beguile us with words – not so successfully perhaps – but can you find any similarities?

Prawn Platter *Prawns on a bed of crisp lettuce masked with brandy laced marie rose sauce*

Magic Mushrooms *Chunky mushrooms in a creamy garlic sauce glazed with fine selected cheese*

Pork Dijonaise *Medallions of roast pork loin napped in a sauce of Dijon and coarse grain mustard and cream*

A Purse of Warm Filo Pastry *with smoked salmon and prawns, dressed on mixed leaves and drizzled with balsamic dressing*

Look at the use of names and the ways words are combined. Think about the difference between a recipe and a menu. Perhaps it's the difference between fact and poetic fiction!

Quiz

1. The poem *Jailbird* likens what to what?

2. Which perfume name  see p 8 suggests something mysterious, dark and ancient?

3. Which toiletry name suggests energy and freshness ▶ see p 8?

4. In his famous statement, to what was Eric Cantona referring when he talked of the seagulls?

5. What do you need to know about Noah in order to understand the joke about leeks ▶ see p 9?

Answers.

1. A prisoner (jailbird) to a real bird

2. primordiale nuit

3. Foamburst Gel

4. the media, reporters, etc.

5. He took animals and presumably plants on to a ship called the Ark before the great Flood.

VARIETY IS THE SPICE OF LIFE – DIFFERENT SORTS OF POETRY

What poems can do
What poetry is
Types of poetry

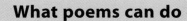

What poems can do

Many people think of poetry as a dreamy activity and have a vision of the poet sitting in a leafy glade, quill in hand, pouring out personal emotions, rather in the manner of these lines by John Keats (1795–1821) perhaps:

My heart aches, and a drowsy numbness pains
My sense, as though of hemlock I had drunk ...

(from **Ode to a Nightingale**, 1819)

DID YOU KNOW

If you read *Ode to a Nightingale* in full, you will discover that it is far from being pure escapism. The poem also contains the chilling lines:

The weariness, the fever, and the fret
Here, where men sit and hear each other groan;
Where palsy shakes a few, sad, last gray hairs,
Where youth grows pale, and specter-thin, and dies

It would be a mistake to regard all poets and their poetry in this way (Incidentally Keats was a down-to-earth Londoner who certainly didn't spend his time reclining in leafy bowers!)

N
O
T
E
S

14

Poems can do much more than vaguely establish a pleasant mood.

DID YOU KNOW?
John Keats didn't start off as a poet — he was a medical student! He was only 26 when he died — of consumption — in Rome.

The weariness, the fever, and the fret.

Poems can among many, many other things:

Be cynical:

The Bed

The doctor loves the patient,
The patient loves his bed;
A fine place to be born in,
The best place to be dead.

The doctor loves the patient
Because he means to die;
The patient loves the patient bed
That shares his agony.

The bed adores the doctor,
His cool and skilful touch
Soon brings another patient
Who loves her just as much.

(A.D. Hope, 1907–)

N
O
T
E
S

Poke fun:

Kindness to Animals

If I went vegetarian
And didn't eat lambs for dinner,
I think I'd be a better person
And also thinner.

But the lamb is not endangered
And least I can truthfully say
I have never, eaten ever a barn owl,
So perhaps I am OK.

(Wendy Cope, 1945–)

Shock:

Does it matter? – losing your leg? ...
For people will always be kind,
And you need not show that you mind
When the others come in after hunting
To gobble their muffins and eggs.

Does it matter? – losing your sight? ...
There's such splendid work for the blind;
And people will always be kind,
As you sit on the terrace remembering
And turning your face to the light.

(from **Does it matter?**, Siegfried Sassoon, 1886–1967)

N
O
T
E
S

DID YOU KNOW?

Poets have been known to write about almost anything. A quick glance through some titles reveals some intriguing subjects: *Breaded Fish* (A.K. Ramanujan, 1966); *Dusting* (Rita Dove, 1986); *A Mud Dauber Wasp* (Peter Kane Dufault, 1978); *Of Green Steps and Laundry* (A.A. Klein, 1977) — the list is endless and certainly not dull!

Or simply amuse (in a slightly wicked way):

The Pizza

Look at itsy-bitsy Mitzi!
See her figure slim and ritzy!
She eatsa
Pizza!
Greedy Mitzi!
She no longer itsy-bitsy!

(Ogden Nash, 1902–71)

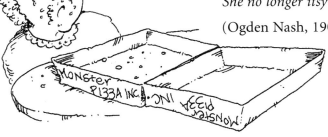

These examples form just a tiny sample of the almost limitless variety that is poetry.

What is poetry?

There is no simple answer to that question but **one essential feature of all poetry is that it is language fashioned and crafted so as to be performed by the human voice.** The oldest forms of poetry were chanted aloud long before they were ever written down. You don't have to frighten the neighbours by bawling out every poem you're studying but do try to 'hear' the verse, even when you are reading silently.

Another important feature is that **poetry is a kind of compressed thought.** If you think of prose writing, in say a newspaper, as laying ideas end to end, poetry can stack them up as well. **A line of poetry may contain much more meaning than the number of words suggest**

For instance, this stanza from *They Shut Me Up in Prose* by Emily Dickinson (1830–86) is only one sentence but it relates simultaneously to her childhood, her physical and imaginative confinement and the difference between prose and poetry:

They shut me up in prose,
As when a little girl
They put me in the closet
Because they liked me 'still'.

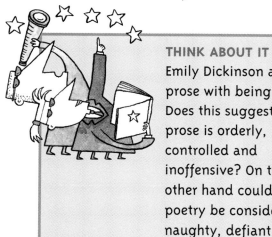

THINK ABOUT IT
Emily Dickinson associates prose with being still. Does this suggest that prose is orderly, controlled and inoffensive? On the other hand could poetry be considered naughty, defiant and unpredictable?

N
O
T
E
S

Types of poetry

Traditionally, poetry was divided into four general types: epic, dramatic, lyric and verse forms.

Epic

This is a long narrative poem (one that tells a story) which deals with a serious subject. This is one of the oldest forms of poetry and the ancient epics such as the *Iliad* and the *Odyssey*, attributed to the Greek poet Homer, told of the exploits of gods and heroes. England has its own traditional epic in the form of the Old English poem, *Beowulf*, probably composed in the eighth century AD. It tells of the exploits of the hero, Beowulf, and how he slew the monster Grendel and then Grendel's mother.

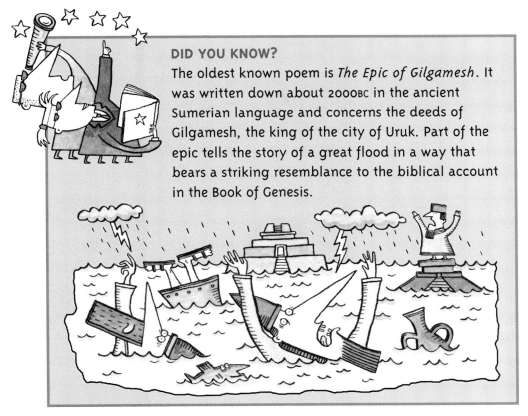

DID YOU KNOW?
The oldest known poem is *The Epic of Gilgamesh*. It was written down about 2000BC in the ancient Sumerian language and concerns the deeds of Gilgamesh, the king of the city of Uruk. Part of the epic tells the story of a great flood in a way that bears a striking resemblance to the biblical account in the Book of Genesis.

In relatively modern times epic poems in English have included Edmund Spenser's *Faerie Queene*, 1590–6, John Milton's Paradise Lost (about 1660–7) and William Wordsworth's *The Prelude* (1798–1800, revised 1850).

In recent times, poets have not aspired to write on such a scale (*The Faerie Queene* runs to over 400 pages!) but Nobel Prize winning West Indian poet, Derek Walcott's *Omeros* (1981) creates a Caribbean epic on the lines of Homer.

Dramatic poetry

This category involves an imagined speaking voice. It includes dramatic monologues like *Porphyria's Lover* ▶ see pp 34–35 and verse drama, such as the plays of Shakespeare which lie outside the scope of this guide. (There is a **York Personal Tutor** on Shakespeare that you may like to look at.)

Lyric poetry

Originally, this was poetry that was performed to the accompaniment of a lyre, an instrument a bit like a harp. Today we still talk of song lyrics. The term is more widely used of a wide variety of short, often intimate poems, usually on a single subject. Poets frequently employ the personal pronoun 'I' in lyric poetry. Most of the poems you are likely to study are strictly speaking, lyric poems.

HIGHER PERFORMANCE

Traditionally lyric poetry has been closely associated with music and love.

In the last 250 years or so, the 'minstrel' or poet musician has largely disappeared, until recently that is with the emergence of figures such as Benjamin Zephaniah whose aim is to 'put poetry into music' and to 'do anything to change the dead, white and boring image of poetry'.

Verse forms

Poets from all periods have tended to choose 'off the peg' verse forms (although that doesn't make writing any easier). There is no need to learn about all the various possibilities in detail but there are a few basic forms that constantly reappear.

- **Blank verse** which does not rhyme and is recognised as being the closest to natural English speech. Shakespeare's plays are written mostly in blank verse.

- **Rhyming verse** of which the rhyming couplet (pairs of lines that rhyme) has a long history from Chaucer to the present day. Rhyming couplets tend to produce a sense of balance within the verse as we tend to anticipate second rhyme that rounds off each couplet.

N
O
T
E
S

DID YOU KNOW?

Satirical poetry — poetry that ridicules people or ideas or general stupidity — is often written in rhyming couplets. Consider this example from *Never Mind the Overcoat* by Ogden Nash (1902–71):

Persons who have something to say like to talk
  about the arts and politics and economics,
And even the cultural aspects of comics.
Among persons who have nothing to say the
  conversational content worsens;
They talk about other persons.

- **The quatrain** is a stanza (or verse) of four lines which may or may not rhyme. It is frequently used in traditional ballads and hymns. It has been most famously used in Samuel Taylor Coleridge's Gothic narrative *The Rime of the Ancient Mariner* (1798) ▶ see p 85

- **The sonnet** is a particularly elaborate but concentrated form and usually involves the close development of an idea. There are several different forms of sonnet but they all involve exactly fourteen iambic pentameters (lines of blank verse with ten syllables).

- **A haiku** is a Japanese verse form. A haiku has seventeen syllables: line 1 has five syllables, line 2 has seven and line 3 has five. It usually concentrates on one idea or observation (there's not much room for more than one subject in that few syllables anyway!) and often describes a natural scene or an object in a way that suggests a particular feeling.

- **Other verse forms** that have fixed rules include tanka, cinquain (borrowed from the Japanese) and limerick.

It's worth finding out about these forms and trying them yourself. They are all very short forms and provide you with a valuable introduction to choosing your words precisely.

NOTES

DID YOU KNOW?

Wendy Cope (1945–) wrote a haiku that is rather less serious than traditional haikus:

*The leaves have fallen
And the snow has fallen too
Soon my hair also...*

- **Free verse** as the term suggests, is not tied to any specific verse form. There are a number of examples in this guide. For example, poems by Philip Larkin see p 74, and Robert Frost see p 57.

N
O
T
E
S

HIGHER PERFORMANCE

There are many, many poems that begin 'If'. Sometimes, as in Wendy Cope's *Kindness to Animals* ▶ **see p 16**, 'if' announces a simple introductory circumstance from which the rest follows quite straightforwardly. Sometimes, however, the word sets up an unusual proposition, a kind of self-created problem that the poet proceeds to solve. Look at the beginning of *Water* by Philip Larkin (1922–85). We ask ourselves how the poet could possibly construct a religion based on water, whilst the poet provokes us into seeing unusual connections. See if you can follow his line of thought:

Water

If I were called in
To construct a religion
I should make use of water.

Going to church
Would entail a fording
To dry, different clothes;

The litany would employ
Images of sousing,
A furious devout drench,

And I should raise in the east
A glass of water
Where any-angled light
Would congregate endlessly.

Quiz

1. In *The Bed* ▶ see p 15 what is the poet suggesting about health care?

2. In *Kindess to Animals* ▶ see p 16 what does Wendy Cope send up?

3. In does It Matter? ▶ see p 16 what does Sassoon feel about the people who will 'always be kind'?

4. What is an essential feature of all poetry?

5. What is one significant difference between poetry and prose (as in newspapers)?

6. What are the three distinctive features of the traditional epic?

7. What is the name of an Old English epic poem?

8. Which modern-day poet wants to 'change the dead, white and boring image of poetry'?

9. Strictly speaking, in what category of poetry does Sassoon's *Does it matter?* ▶ see p 16 fall?

10. What is the most obvious feature of blank verse?

Answers

1 That it is impersonal and lacks any lasting relationships

2 Vegetarians, animal lovers, middle-class values and herself

3 They are complacent and do not really care.

4 It is language crafted so that it can be performed by the human voice.

5 Prose tends to present ideas in a sequence, whereas poetry can suggest more than one idea at once.

6 It is long, narrative and concerns the actions of great heroes.

7 *Beowulf*

8 Benjamin Zephaniah

9 Lyric poetry

10 It does not rhyme.

WHAT'S IT ALL ABOUT?
– MEANING IN POETRY

Narrative poetry

Descriptive poetry

The narrator

'What is it about?' is one of the simplest and most natural questions to ask, but is sometimes the most difficult to answer. **Some poems convey more meaning than may first strike the eye.** There is often a difference between subject-matter and meaning.

First, poetry, unlike prose, is rarely concerned with recording factual information for its own sake. Poets are not aiming to repeat what newspapers, history books and encyclopaedias do so well. Even purely narrative poetry amounts to something rather different from what a novel or short story offers.

Poets try to make sense of the world by responding to it in fresh and sometimes startling ways. **Poets never take anything at face value; they see things differently.** They may engage our emotions, exercise our minds, illuminate the commonplace or imagine the unimaginable.

Secondly, it is important to draw a distinction between a poem's literal subject-matter and what it is really 'about'.

THINK ABOUT IT

Ask yourself what a football match is 'about'. As one 'legendary' manager, Bill Shankly, famously put it: 'Some people believe football is a matter of life and death, I am disappointed with that attitude. I can assure you it is much, much more important than that.'

Narrative Poetry

The following three examples are all 'about' matters to do with war but the thoughts and feelings they convey are quite different.

A poem with a 'message'

At the Cenotaph

I saw the Prince of Darkness, with his Staff,
Standing bare-headed by the Cenotaph:
Unostentatious and respectful, there
He stood, and offered up the following prayer.
'Make them forget, O Lord, what this Memorial
Means; their discredited ideas revive;
Breed new belief that War is purgatorial
Proof of the pride and power of being alive;
Men's biologic urge to readjust
The Map of Europe, Lord of Hosts, increase;
Lift up their hearts in large destructive lust;
And crown their heads with blind vindictive Peace.'
The Prince of Darkness to the Cenotaph
Bowed. As he walked away I heard him laugh.

(Siegfried Sassoon, 1886–1967)

NOTES

27

- On the face of it, the scene resembles something out of a horror film!

- The poem, a sonnet see p 22, tells us that the Devil stands paying his respects at a ceremony of remembrance for those who had died in the war. He prays that people will soon forget and turn to war once again. Then, with a laugh, he walks away.

- That is roughly the poem's literal sense and if you leave it at that, you might conclude that the poet is simply suggesting there are always dark forces at work in our midst ready to wage war.

But think about these questions:

- Why are the Devil's henchmen referred to as 'Staff'?
  It is the generals who have 'Staff' (the capital letter is important here). It is they who stand 'respectfully' but no less proud of military tradition than before the war.

- Why is the Devil 'unostentatious' and 'respectful'?
  Sassoon was being consciously satirical see p 22 by undermining our conventional assumptions.

- Why does he laugh?
  He is suggesting the ceremony that is supposed to remember the dead is, in fact, paying homage to war.

KEY CONCEPTS

※ No poet wants to say the obvious in an obvious way — anyone can do that

※ 'Great literature is simply language charged with meaning to the utmost possible meaning.' Ezra Pound

※ We often need to look beyond the literal meaning of a poem to what is being suggested or implied

N
O
T
E
S

A poem with a story

Everyone enjoys a good story and for the most part what a narrative poem is about and the literal meaning are closely connected. But even the most factual narrative poem does more than simply record events.

In this extract from a history book called *The Reason Why* (1896), Cecil Woodham-Smith describes a famous incident in the Crimean War:

General Scarlett, in command of the Heavy Brigade, assisted by his two advisers, was now to perform what has been called 'one of the great feats of cavalry against cavalry in the history of Europe'.

The Russian cavalry were 3,000 to 4,000 strong, and the effect of such a body of horsemen in a disciplined mass is overwhelming. They were only a few hundred yards away, and they were on the slope above General Scarlett. Nevertheless, Scarlett gave the order to wheel into line. Though his eight squadrons numbered only about 500 troopers he intended to charge the thousands before him, and charge uphill.

Alfred Lord Tennyson (1809–92) wrote of the same event in his 1885 poem *The Charge of the Heavy Brigade at Balaclava October 25, 1854*:

The charge of the gallant three hundred, the Heavy Brigade!
Down the hill, down the hill, thousands of Russians,
Thousands of horsemen, drew to the valley – and stay'd;
For Scarlett and Scarlett's three hundred were riding by
When the points of the Russian lances arose in the sky;
And he call'd 'Left wheel into line!' and they wheel'd and obey'd.
Then he look'd at the host that had halted he knew not why,
And he turn'd half round, and bad he his trumpeter sound
To the charge, and he rode on ahead, as he waved his blade
To the gallant three hundred whose glory will never die–
'Follow', and up the hill, up the hill, up the hill,
Follow'd the Heavy Brigade.

- Factually, the two accounts are very similar; the subject-matter and the literal meaning of both extracts are pretty well identical.

- Which is the more memorable, however? The first provides the facts but the poem provides the colour. The poet tries to recapture the drama and excitement of the event through the use of powerful rhythm and devices such as repetition ◉ **see p 57**. He celebrates the action and the poem is as much about extraordinary heroism as it is about a particular battle.

- Furthermore, it may be said that the tone, or mood of the poem reflects public attitudes towards the end of the last century, which tended to regard prowess on the battlefield as a matter of honour and national prestige.

DID YOU KNOW?
Cardigans and balaclavas were first worn during the Crimean war to keep the troops warm. Cardigans were named after the seventh Earl of Cardigan, leader of the Light Brigade, and balaclava helmets were named after the 1854 Battle of Balaclava.

An ironic poem

The scene of war: the happy warrior

His wild heart beats with painful sobs
his stain'd hands clench an ice-cold rifle
his aching jaws grip a hot parch'd tongue
his wide eyes search unconsciously.

He cannot shriek

Bloody saliva
dribbles down his shapeless jacket.

I saw him stab
and stab again
a well-killed Boche.

This is the happy warrior,
this is he ...

(Herbert Read, 1893–1968)

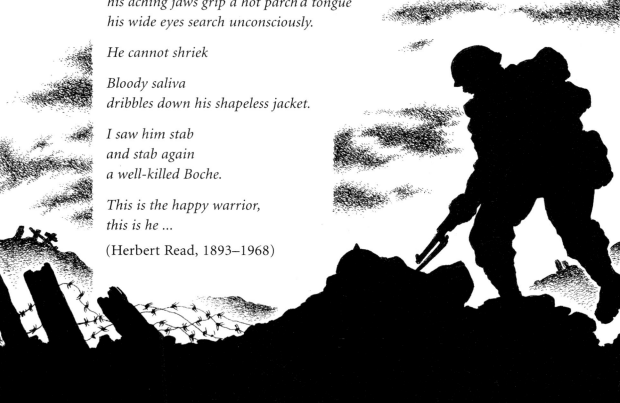

- At first, the poem appears to be a matter of direct observation on the battlefield; we see the soldier and his actions.

- But the poem is not really about this particular soldier as such. The key word is 'happy'. What does it mean here? How could the soldier be happy in such appalling conditions?

- The word is, of course, used ironically. We see only a person numbed senseless by the terrible conditions. He is 'happy' only insofar as he now knows no different.

NOTES

Descriptive poetry

We almost expect poetry to be descriptive. However, even the simplest description may have a deeper significance.

THINK ABOUT IT

Even the greatest poets can have feet of clay. William Wordsworth's description of a mountain pool in *The Thorn* (1798), is rather less than poetic!

And to the left, three yards beyond,
You see a little muddy pond
Of water, never dry,
I've measured it from side to side:
'Tis three feet long and two feet wide.

Perhaps to cover his embarrassment, the poet later revised the last two lines to:

Though but of compass small, and bare
To thirsty suns and parching air.

The next poem appears to be 'about' a dead butterfly, but equally it suggests something about the fragility of life and the impermanence of beauty.

The butterfly's colourings are compared to the stones of the city. A butterfly is the embodiment of delicate, fragile beauty. The stones suggest solidity and permanence. By associating the two, the poet may be suggesting that these contrasting qualities merge and interpenetrate in some way. Perhaps human affairs are less significant, less rock-like, than we like to believe and the fleeting vision of the butterfly, for ever reappearing in the natural cycle, is something we should cherish and preserve.

N O T E S

The Dead Butterfly

Now I see its whiteness
is not white but green, traced with green,
and resembles the stones,
of which the city is built,
quarried high in the mountains.

Everywhere among the marigolds
the rainblown roses and the hedges
of tamarisk are white
butterflies this morning, in constant
tremulous movement, only those
that lie dead revealing
their rockgreen colour and the bold
cut of the wings.

(Denise Levertov, 1923–)

KEY CONCEPTS

Appearances can be deceptive ✳

Poets often look for significance in simple things ✳

The particular scene, situation or person that the poet describes may suggest something about life in general ✳

N
O
T
E
S

The deceptive 'I'

One of the most common words in poetry is 'I' but it may also be the most misleading. Do not assume that because the poem is written in the first person, it is necessarily the poet who is speaking or assume that the first person is the most reliable source of information.

You need to distinguish between the writer and the narrator – the voice 'telling' the poem.

Let's look at a poem by Robert Browning (1812–90):

Porphyria's Lover

The rain set early in to-night,
The sullen wind was soon awake,
It tore the elm-tops down for spite,
And did its worst to vex the lake:
I listened with heart fit to break.
When glided in Porphyria; straight
She shut the cold out and the storm,
And kneeled and made the cheerless grate
Blaze up, and all the cottage warm;
Which done, she rose, and from her form
Withdrew the dripping cloak and shawl,
And laid her soiled gloves by, untied
Her hat and let the damp hair fall,
And, last, she sat down by my side
And called me. When no voice replied,
She put my arm about her waist,
And made her smooth white shoulder bare,
And all her yellow hair displaced,
And, stooping, made my cheek lie there,
And spread, o'er all, her yellow hair,
Murmuring how she loved me – she
Too weak, for all her heart's endeavor,
To set its struggling passion free
From pride, and vainer ties dissever,
And give herself to me for ever.

But passion sometimes would prevail,
Nor could to-night's gay feast restrain
A sudden thought of one so pale
For love of her, and all in vain:
So, she was come through wind and rain.
Be sure I looked up at her eyes
Happy and proud; at last I knew
Porphyria worshipped me: surprise
Made my heart swell, and still it grew
While I debated what to do.
That moment she was mine, mine, fair,
Perfectly pure and good: I found
A thing to do, and all her hair
In one long yellow string I wound
Three times her little throat around,
And strangled her. No pain felt she;
I am quite sure she felt no pain.
As a shut bud that holds a bee,
I warily oped her lids: again
Laughed the blue eyes without a stain.
And I untightened next the tress
About her neck; her cheek once more
Blushed bright beneath my burning kiss:
I propped her head up as before,
Only, this time my shoulder bore
Her head, which droops upon it still:
The smiling rosy little head,
So glad it has its utmost will,
That all it scorned at once is fled,
And I, its love, am gained instead!
Porphyria's love: she guessed not how
Her darling one wish would be heard.
And thus we sit together now,
And all night long we have not stirred,
And yet God has not said a word!

- The literal facts are clear. The narrator sits alone in his room on a stormy night. Porphyria arrives, makes the fire, takes off her wet things and sits beside him. She murmurs her love for the narrator, who remains silent. Eventually he strangles her with her own hair and spends the remainder of the night sitting with her head on his shoulder.

- As important as what the narrator says is *how* he says it. His account is delivered in a matter-of-fact way. He records killing Porphyria in three blunt words, 'And strangled her'. How could a man kill the woman he loves and talk of the murder so calmly?

- The narrator seems to rationalise his actions with calm detachment. In fact, after he has killed her, she seems more alive to him than before.

- To whom is this account addressed? Is it to someone who has discovered the scene? Is he justifying his actions to himself?

- He seems compelled to explain but does his account, which seems so clear, really uncover his motives? Is he afraid of Porphyria? Does he feel betrayed by her?

- The poem's skill lies in no small part in the fact that, although the narrator appears to speak absolutely candidly, we do not quite know in what way to understand him.

By contrast, the following poem, one of the most moving in the English language, is unusual in that it gives direct access to the deeply disturbed mind. It was written by John Clare (1793–1864) towards the end of his life when he was confined in Northampton General Lunatic Asylum. Poetry was his last, faltering grasp on reality. He could write for no one but himself and in this case the 'I' of the title is the mind of the man himself.

Think about what the simple words 'I am' mean to you.

I AM

I AM: yet what I am none cares or knows,
My friends forsake me like a memory lost;
I am the self-consumer of my woes,
They rise and vanish in oblivious host,
Like shades in love and death's oblivion lost;
And yet I am, and live with shadows tost

Into the nothingness of scorn and noise,
Into the living sea of waking dreams,
Where there is neither sense of life nor joys,
But the vast shipwreck of my life's esteems;
And e'en the dearest – that I loved the best –
Are strange – nay, rather stranger than the rest.

I long for scenes where man has never trod,
A place where woman never smiled or wept;
There to abide with my Creator, God,
And sleep as I in childhood sweetly slept:
Untroubling and untroubled where I lie,
The grass below – above the vaulted sky.

THINK ABOUT IT

A letter, written at about the same time as *I Am*, reveals the poet's collapse into mental chaos:

> DEAR SIR,
>
> – I am in a Madhouse & quite forget your Name or who you are. You must excuse me for I have nothing to communicate or tell & why I am shut up I don't know I have nothing to say so I conclude
>
> Yours respectfully
> JOHN CLARE

HIGHER PERFORMANCE

1 Look again at *Porphyria's Lover* ▶ **see pp 34–35**. When we encounter this poem we are naturally fascinated by the mind of the narrator and his obsession. If, however, we shift our point of view we may discover quite a lot about Porphyria. Look at the evidence of her appearance and behaviour. What can you find out about her? What is her background? Why has she come? Where from?

2 In this little poem, the Nigerian writer, Odia Ofeimun, reflects on the first landing on the Moon, although there is no direct mention of any details of the event. Should Ofeimun's call for celebration be taken at face value?

Landing on the Moon
Gobble the news with seven grains
of alligator pepper, a pinch of salt,
white chalk, one sea-deep cry
for man's hike to Jehovah-hood, or,
must we not submerge in rituals
this explosive moment of animal triumph? –
Catch my hand, brother
we are annexing the kingdom of the gods.

(Odia Ofeimun)

Quiz

1. On which ceremony is *At the Cenotaph*  see p 27 based?

2. In *At the Cenotaph* with whom does the poet identify the Devil?

3. Why does the Devil pray that men will read just the Map of Europe?

4. In what point of fact do the two accounts differ concerning the size of the Heavy Brigade see p 29?

5. In Tennyson's *The Charge of the Heavy Brigade* see p 29 'Down the hill, down the hill' is an example of what device?

6. In *The Happy Warrior* see p 31 the poet is suggesting that the soldier:

a. enjoys fighting

b. hates the enemy

c. no longer has any feelings

d. respects his superiors

Which is the correct answer?

7. In *The Dead Butterfly* see p 33 which word describes the butterflies' quivering flight?

8. In *I Am* see p 37, which two lines tells us that Clare is unable to share his pain with anyone?

9. What line suggests that Clare had an unhappy marriage?

WEIRD AND WONDERFUL WORDS – WHAT WORDS DO

Nonsense verse
Connotation
Metaphor and simile

Let's look at how poets use words. In particular, the importance of connotation, the extra meaning that a word generates beyond its literal meaning. Unless you are alert to what words suggest, the point of many poems may be lost.

Delight in words is at the heart of poetry. The Old English poets referred to their 'word hoard', as though it was a treasure chest containing precious jewels. For poets – and it is to be hoped their readers – words hold an endless fascination.

Sense or Nonsense?

'Twas brillig, and the slithy toves
Did gyre and gimble in the wabe:
All mimsy were the borogoves,
And the mome raths outgrabe.

'Beware the Jabberwock, my son!
The jaws that bite, the claws that catch!
Beware the Jubjub bird, and shun
The frumious Bandersnatch!'

(from **Jabberwocky**, 1871)

N
O
T
E
S

40

Nonsense poetry helps us to appreciate that words can do much more than convey straightforward meaning.

You may well know *Jabberwocky* from *Through the Looking Glass* by Lewis Carroll (Charles Lutwidge Dodgson, 1832–98). Alice finds the poem lying on a table. At first she cannot make head or tail of it as it appears to be written in a strange script, but even when she realises that it can be read with the aid of a mirror, it still doesn't make much sense.

Of course, words such as 'brillig', 'slithy' and 'toves' don't exist in normal English. Yet all the strange words do make a peculiar kind of sense; as Alice remarks, 'It seems to fill my head with ideas – only I don't know exactly what they are.'

We respond to the poem because, although the nonsense words do not have any familiar meaning, they do seem to strike home. Humpty Dumpty explained some of the words to Alice:

....

'Brillig' means four o'clock in the afternoon – when you begin broiling things for dinner.'

'That'll do very well,' said Alice: 'and "slithy"?'

'Well, "slithy" means "lithe and slimy". "Lithe" is the same as "active". You see it's like a portmanteau – there are two meanings packed up into one word.'

....

DID YOU KNOW?
If you ever 'chortle' or call the day 'frabjous' (meaning delightful or joyous) you will be using nonsense words by Lewis Carroll that have passed into our language.

The 'jabberwocky' effect!

The poem that follows is not a nonsense poem at all but, like Lewis Carroll, the poet uses words in a very special way: he attempts to find an equivalent in words of an experience or sensation. Gerard Manley Hopkins (1844–89) wrote *Inversnaid* in 1881, just ten years after the publication of *Through the Looking Glass*. These first two stanzas don't so much describe a mountain stream as attempt to recreate the feeling of the torrent from its beginning to the point at which it plunges into a pool:

This darksome burn, horseback brown,
His rollrock highroad roaring down,
In coop and in comb the fleece of his foam
Flutes and low to the lake falls home.

A windpuff-bonnet of fáwn-fróth
Turns and twindles over the broth
Of a pool so pitchblack, féll-frówning,
It rounds and rounds Despair to drowning.

(from **Inversnaid**, 1881)

There is a thread of conventional sense, insofar as the poet registers the progress of the stream down the mountain side, but what is most striking is the use of original and unusual words and phrases, such as 'rollrock highroad', 'windpuff-bonnet', 'fáwn-fróth', 'féll-frówning'. These create clusters of meaning, which are untranslatable. For example, the phrase 'rollrock highroad' combines the ideas of a rocky mountain water and the sense of the stream wrapping itself around the boulders. In some indefinable way, the phrase 'rollrock' also seems to embody the sense of weight and shape.

Incidentally 'twindles' may be an example of Humpty Dumpty's portmanteaux words, perhaps a combination of 'twist' and 'dwindle'.

N O T E S

Connotation

As well as the principal sense, words have secondary meanings, overtones and associations – connotations. What a word *suggests* may even be more important than the meaning!

Let's look at a famous poem by William Blake (1757–1827):

The Tyger

Tyger Tyger burning bright,
In the forests of the night;
What immortal hand or eye,
Could frame thy fearful symmetry?

In what distant deeps or skies,
Burnt the fire of thine eyes?
On what wings dare he aspire?
What the hand, dare seize the fire?

And what shoulder, and what art,
Could twist the sinews of thy heart?
And when thy heart began to beat,
What dread hand? And what dread feet?

What the hammer? what the chain,
In what furnace was thy brain?
What the anvil? what dread grasp
Dare its deadly terrors clasp?

When the stars threw down their spears,
And water'd heaven with their tears:
Did he smile his work to see?
Did he who made the Lamb make thee?

Tyger Tyger burning bright,
In the forests of the night:
What immortal hand or eye,
Dare frame thy fearful symmetry?

N
O
T
E
S

The poem has always had an almost hypnotic effect on readers but at the same time been notoriously difficult to explain. We can, however, find out a lot about its nature simply by considering the suggestiveness of its vocabulary.

- **Tyger** as well as meaning a particular species of animal, 'tyger' conjures up images of untamed ferocity and of mystery

- **burning** suggests passion as well as glowing in the dark

- **bright** combined with burning suggests intensity but also draws in associations of light, of something shining gloriously

- **forests** are not only wild places, they are mysterious places which are dark and impenetrable

- **night** has multiple associations with evil, fear and mystery and in this context we also imagine the two burning eyes in the darkness

You can probably think of more associations of your own and as you do so you will become aware of how Blake builds up a mosaic of sense and feeling.

As one moves through the poem patterns of contrasting emotions and associations begin to take root:

- **distant** may suggest the unimaginable as well as merely far away

- **burnt** can be read in two ways: either in the sense that the tiger's eyes were burning or that an unknown power burnt the fire into the tiger's eyes. Either way, the words suggest power, energy, even violence

- **Twist, hammer, chain, furnace, anvil** convey feelings of force and violence but have specific associations of beating white hot metal into shape

- **Lamb** is most obviously associated with innocence and gentleness; it contrasts with the image of the tiger but it is also a reference to Jesus Christ, the Lamb of God

These are just some of the possible connotations of the words, or diction, of Tyger. Of course, each reader will respond to the words in a personal way and we also know that many of the terms in the poem had special meaning for Blake.

Quite how the words and their connotations combine to create the poem's meaning is a matter for repeated reading and interpretation (and few poems have had so many!) but it is the strength of poetry that it can communicate even if one cannot fully understand it. If you allow Blake's vocabulary to play on your imagination, you will absorb much of the poem's force.

DID YOU KNOW?
William Blake was better known in his day as an artist and engraver. In *The Tyger* 'forests of the night' may have been, among all else, a reference to the production of charcoal necessary to the process of making the plates for engraving and 'hammer' and 'furnace' were also probably familiar to the engraver.

Come and see my etchings

Establishing a mood

It's sometimes helpful to consider how the vocabulary of a poem is 'loaded'. A useful test is to divide the principal words into rough categories, such as,

– words that create broadly pleasant or positive images
– words that create broadly unpleasant or negative images

In case you think that poets are always being miserable, Vernon Scannell (1922–)presents a contented view of the world:

View from a deckchair

I rest in the canvas lap and let fall my book.
The breeze, browsing, flips a few pages,
Leaves it, then comes back for a second look.
My eyelids close, like mouths, on the images.

The sky is green with the smell of crunched grass
Whose dark, shed juice seasons the simmering air;
Eyelids slide open, eyes see a butterfly pass,
Pause, wings frittering, treading the air's water.

Summer mothers me; here I feel secure;
My neighbours are not likely to break down the fences;
The only guns they carry are for making war
On garden pests. Their televisions have valid licences.

Vapour-trails, squeezed out on the bland blue,
Perturb only slightly; the bee's buzz does not sting.
Even when a motorbike rasps in the avenue
The heart bucks only a little, and I stay sitting,

Or, rather, reclining in my garden chair,
And can stay here for at least another hour
Before the benevolent and grass-flavoured air
Loses its warmth, and the chill tastes sour.

If we examine the poem, we see how the poet 'weights' his vocabulary.

Snarl words	break down / perturb / guns / war / pests / sting / rasps / chill / sour	9
Purr words	green / crunched grass? (probably) / dark … juice / simmering / butterfly / frittering / mothers / secure / bland blue / bee's buzz / reclining / benevolent / grass-flavoured / warmth	14
Neutral words	canvas / lap / fall / book / second look / eyelids / images / pass / treading / licences / vapour-trails / motor-bike / avenue / sitting / garden chair / hour / air	17

It can be hard to decide in which category to put the words but the most important feature here is that no words are really very 'snarly'. Even 'guns' and 'war' are quite innocent in this context and, in fact, the poet specifically uses the words in the snarl column to reinforce his positive enjoyment (e.g. 'My neighbours are not likely to break down the fences'). The poem is after all, about contentment and being at peace with the world, at least for an afternoon!

THINK ABOUT IT

It is vital to judge the effect of each word in its context. Words have no single, fixed meaning neither do they have fixed connotations. For instance, 'dark' usually has sinister connotations but when Vernon Scannell refers to the 'dark, shed juice', it takes on connotations of richness, unless, of course you have a particular dislike of the smell of mown grass.

Metaphor and simile

This ability to make comparisons finds its clearest expression in metaphor and simile. Basically, as you probably know; a metaphor is a *figure of speech* which involves an *unstated* comparison 'He was a lion on the battlefield.' and a simile (note the spelling – plural **similes**) involves a direct comparison, usually using 'like', 'as' or 'than' 'He fought like a lion on the battlefield.'

Metaphor and simile are frequently referred to as *imagery*.

In *Holy-Cross Day* by Robert Browning (1812–89), the persecuted Jews describe their condition in a succession of metaphorical comparisons:

Higgledy piggledy, packed we lie,
Rats in a hamper, swine in a stye,
Wasps in a bottle, frogs in a sieve,
Worms in a carcase, fleas in a sleeve.

In *By the Fireside*, the same poet showed that he could turn his hand to a vivid simile:

That crimson the creeper's leaf across
Like a splash of blood, intense, abrupt ...

In *Up at a Villa – Down in the City*, he combines metaphor and simile in the same phrase (examine it carefully):

Except yon cypress that points like death's
lean lifted forefinger.

N
O
T
E
S

DID YOU KNOW?

An essential feature of metaphor and simile is that they compare things that appear to be unlike.
In the seventeenth century there was a vogue for making outrageous and far-fetched comparisons. For example without the title of the poem, it would be difficult to guess what the poet, Richard Lovelace (1618–57), meant when he wrote:

Thou snowy farm with thy five tenements!

The title of Lovelace's poem is *Ellinda's Glove*. (Think about it!)

KEY CONCEPTS

Metaphors and similes are not added to the meaning of a poem. They create meaning ✳

A simile uses 'as' or 'like' ✳

A metaphor is a direct comparison without 'as' or 'like' ✳

NOTES

Poetry is different from ordinary language: poets use metaphor and simile in fresh and stimulating ways often challenging us to see things afresh.

The importance of metaphor for our well-being is explored in an interesting way by D.J. Enright (1920–) in the next poem. We are asked to consider the imagination of a young child who, wide-eyed, sees a peacock for the first time. The child doesn't know what it is called: it is simply a blue umbrella:

Blue Umbrellas

'The thing that makes a blue umbrella with its tail –
How do you call it?' you ask. Poorly and pale
Comes my answer. For all I can call it is peacock.
Now that you go to school, you will learn how we call all sorts
of things;
How we mar great works by our mean recital.
You will learn, for instance, that Head Monster is not the
gentleman's accepted title;
The blue-tailed eccentrics will be merely peacocks; the dead
bird will no longer doze
Off till tomorrow's lark, for the letter has killed him.
The dictionary is opening, the gay umbrellas close.

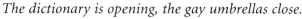

DID YOU KNOW?
In Victorian times it was considered bad luck to bring peacock feathers into the house because it was believed that somebody in the household would then die. Some people still believe this today.

The point the poet is conveying is the preciousness of the child's imagination. The young child's world is constructed out of vibrant images. To the child, the peacock is not a bird with a fan-like tail; it *is* a blue umbrella, a living metaphor. When the children go to school, however, they learn what things are 'properly' called and they cease to look at things imaginatively. The blue umbrella becomes a peacock; the metaphor is replaced with a label.

You may say 'That's life!' but the poem's message, partly at least, is that metaphor is more than a way of describing something. It is a way of understanding and experiencing. For good poets at least, imagery is a way of exploring experience in a fresh way, not just decoration.

KEY CONCEPTS

Words have connotations and associations above and beyond their dictionary meaning. Connotation is a vital ingredient of poetry ✳

Within a poem words may be 'weighted' to present a favourable or unfavourable impression ✳

Poets are constantly finding connections and making comparisons. Simile and metaphor (imagery) are central ways of drawing comparisons ✳

N
O
T
E
S

HIGHER PERFORMANCE

Emily Brontë is most famous for her novel, *Wuthering Heights* (1848) but she also wrote quite a bit of verse. Much of it is fragmentary and comprises brief observations on the weather and her reactions to it. In these two verses how is her mood reflected in her vocabulary? Concentrate on the use of connotation.

Cold, clear, and blue, the morning heaven
Expands its arch on high;
Cold, clear, and blue, Lake Werna's water
Reflects that winter's sky.
The moon has set, but Venus shines
A silent, silvery star.

The old church tower and garden wall
Are black with autumn rain,
And dreary wind foreboding call
The darkness down again.

I watched how evening took the place
Of glad and glorious day;
I watched a deeper gloom efface
The evening's lingering ray.

And as I gazed on the cheerless sky
Sad thoughts rose in my mind ...

Quiz

1. What did Old English poets call their stock of words?

2. What term does Humpty Dumpty, use to define a word like slithy which is made up of two other words like 'lithe' and 'slimy'?

3. In the extract from *Inversnaid* see p 42, which word seems to be a portmanteau word?

4. Pick out the four words in *The Tyger* see p 43 which may be a direct reference to violent industrial processes.

5. What term is used for the additional thoughts and feelings that we connect with words, for example dark = evil?

6. In *View from a Deckchair* see p 46 what phrase compares a butterfly's flight to a kind of swimming?

7. In the quotation from *Up at a Villa – Down in the City* see p 48 what words form
   a. the simile
   b the metaphor?

8. What precisely are 'thy five tenements' referred to in the line from *Ellinda's Glove* see p 49?

9. In *Blue Umbrellas* see p 50, apart from those words, what other phrase springs from the child's imagination?

Answers

1 Word hoard
2 portmanteau
3 twindles
4 hammer, chain, furnace, anvil
5 Connotation
6 treading the air's water
7 a) yon cypress like death's... b) death's lean lifted forefinger
8 the fingers of the glove
9 Head Monster

ALL THAT TECHNICAL STUFF – RHYTHM, RHYME AND MORE

Approaching a poem
Rhyme schemes
Metre

This section looks at the technical aspects of poetry. In particular, it concentrates on the sounds of poetry and the use of rhythm. You should first listen and appreciate how poetry sounds and only then use technical understanding to explain what you hear

Approaching a poem

Unfortunately, one of the most off-putting aspects of studying poetry is having to grapple with the details of how it is written; such matters as rhythm (spelling the word is tricky enough!), rhyme (a bit easier) and all sorts of other things like alliteration and onomatopoeia.

In this section we look at some ways in which poems weave sound patterns in words but first of all, a little advice:

- First of all put your notes in a drawer and approach the poem with an open mind

- Read the poem to yourself, preferably aloud and 'listen' to it, trying not to think too much about its meaning

- Look out for any repeated sounds or any changes in speed that you have to make. It can be helpful to try saying the poem in a monotonous voice; the strain will often reveal what the words are really doing

How poetry is organised

When you read a newspaper or magazine, your eye swings from side to side, working its way down the page. You pay little or no attention to what the words sound like or how they are arranged on the page. Poetry is different – it is organised into lines and frequently into verses or stanzas and, as we shall see, these shapes are not just to please the eye but relate to how the poem sounds to the ear.

Basically there are three interconnecting elements to consider:
1   Rhythm and metre
2   Sound patterns, of which rhyme is the most familiar
3   The organisation into lines

1   Rhythm and metre

These two terms are related and their meanings often overlap.

Rhythm (watch the spelling: **R**ejoice **H**eartily **Y**our **T**eacher **H**as **M**easles!) generally refers to the alternation of stressed and unstressed syllables (see below).

Metre (from a Greek word *metron* meaning 'a measure') refers to a particular pattern or number of stresses in a line, or even part of a line, rather like beats in a bar of music.

In practice, you will probably find it most useful to think simply of a poem's rhythm. To understand this, we must first think about what English is like and how we speak it.

English is an 'accented' language. By that we mean that the name 'Mary', for example, has a greater stress on the first syllable than the second – **Ma**ry. By contrast, in the name 'Marie' the stress is reversed – Ma**rie**. Choose any word of more than one syllable and you will easily see where the main stress lies: **po**etry, ex**cite**ment, **bore**dom, con**fu**sion, etc**et**era.

We do not speak in a flat, even way. Our speech has a rhythm that is created by stressing some syllables more than others. Although we don't consciously plan it, the stresses are fairly regular, so we come to anticipate when the next stress should be.

Once you have grasped how English has its own natural stress patterns or rhythms, it is easier to see how poets turn them to their advantage by organising them into patterns.

The most obvious kind of poetic metre is one that has a very regular rhythm.

Nursery rhymes always have a very clear, strong rhythm:

Máry hád a líttle lámb,
Its fléece was whíte as snów;
And éverywhére that Máry wént,
The lámb was súre to gó.

In that familiar verse, the rhythm is regular and easy to sense because it alternates stressed and relatively unstressed syllables. Look (or listen) more closely, however and you will notice that even this simple verse is not entirely uniform. The first line leads off with a stressed syllable, whereas the other lines begin with an unstressed syllable so that the rhythm is reversed and **tum**-ti (**Ma**-ry) becomes ti-**tum** (Its-**fleece**).

The posh word for the ti-**tum** rhythm is *iambic*.

The **tum**-ti rhythm is known as *trochaic*.

There are many other patterns, including:
anapaestic – ti-ti-**tum** and *dactylic* – **tum**-ti-ti

DID YOU KNOW?

Iambus comes with steady pace.
Swift the trochee takes its place
Then comes the dactyl with pattering feet
The amphibrach next with its swift middle beat.
And last but not least is the rare anapaest.
(Sarah McCombie 1957–)

In the following examples, the poets have used repeated words which create a very clear stress pattern.

Compare the different effects that are produced. For instance, you may be able to see how Milton's hammer blow stresses ('Dárk, dárk, dárk …') are tied in with the blind Samson's agonised despair. By contrast, the gentle iambic (ti-**tum**) tread of the repeated lines in the poem by Robert Frost seem to chime with a sense of calm weariness as evening closes in on a peaceful winter's day.

O dark, dark, dark, amid the blaze of noon,
Irrecoverably dark, total eclipse
Without all hope of day!

(from **Samson Agonistes** byJohn Milton, 1608–74)

The woods are lovely, dark and deep,
But I have promises to keep,
And miles to go before I sleep,
And miles to go before I sleep.

(from **Stopping by Woods on a Snowy Evening** byRobert Frost, 1874–1963)

About feet! – but not too much.

Books on poetry usually have long sections on how lines are divided into so-called feet, rather like bars in music.

The example always quoted is the iambic pentameter. This is a ten-syllable line which divides neatly into five little iambs:

*What **oft** / was **thought** / but **ne'er** / so **well** / ex**press'd** /*

(from **Essay on Criticism** by Alexander Pope, 1688–1744)

John Milton (1608–74) wrote *Paradise Lost* all in iambic pentameters (10,602 of them, in fact!).

DID YOU KNOW?

Shakespeare's plays are written almost entirely in iambic pentameters. The challenge for the actor is how to produce believable dramatic emphasis whilst paying attention to the poetic rhythm.

For instance, in *Richard III*, the Duchess of York was not referring to her English teacher when she uttered these words:

Thou cam'st on earth to make the earth my hell.
A grievous burden was thy birth to me;

The lines are in absolutely regular iambic rhythm, but how do you say them so as to bring out feeling of the words?

When you look at more modern poetry, you find that the question of division into feet is often irrelevant, as it is frequently written in so-called *free verse* and does not obey the traditional rules. Yet when you read this little poem by William Carlos Williams (1883–1963), you'll still sense a careful organisation of the stresses:

The Loving Dexterity

The flower
    fallen
she saw it

    where
it lay
    a pink petal

intact
    deftly
placed it

    on
its stem
    again

The metre or rhythmical patterning of poetry is like flower arranging: there may be a satisfying sense of shape and balance without slavish regularity.

DID YOU KNOW?

In some poetry, the verse rhythms may be much stronger than the natural speech rhythms. This is especially noticeable when the poetry is closely associated with music. Many modern West Indian poets, for instance, build on the Caribbean folk tradition, blending natural speech forms and the style of folk song:

an de beat well red
an de scene well dread
an de man dem a loot
an shoot.
        Laaard!
an de fia bun
an de blod a run
an some people jus doan
know weh fe tun
an de politicians a preach
an de preachas a pray
but tings a get worse
day after day

(from **Reflection in Red,** Oku Onoura, 1952—)

Finding out about rhythms and patterns for yourself

One more technical term: Working out the rhythmical patterns in poetry is called scansion. Scanning a line of poetry is most of the time a pretty pointless activity in itself, but our enjoyment of poetry depends on our feeling of satisfaction when the verse scans, that is, stresses properly fit together.

DID YOU KNOW?

An old-fashioned word for writing in verse is 'numbers'. The idea of counting which the word suggests, is useful when poets choose not to base their writing on strict stress patterns. *Considering the Snail* by Thom Gunn (1929–) has no obvious rhythm but has exactly seven syllables in each line, so that they all carry the same 'weight', as it were. Here's a verse:

The snail pushes through a green
night, for the grass is heavy
with water and meets over
the bright path he makes, where rain
has darkened the earth's dark. He
moves in a wood of desire,

One way to appreciate how verse scans is look at what happens when it doesn't! Try this test. Sing a verse of the familiar Lennon and McCartney song *Yesterday* to yourself (or anyone else who can stand it).

Yesterday, all my troubles seemed so far away
Now it looks as though they're here to stay
Oh, I believe in yesterday.

Now try doing the same with a slightly altered text.

Last week, all my difficulties were a long way away,
Today I think that they have returned to stay,
Oh, I trust in yesterday.

If you are unable to make the words fit the tune, can you work out where the second version goes wrong? You will discover that particular words are too long or too short to fit the natural beat of the tune. In other words, the verse doesn't scan.

NOTES

You may wish to amuse yourself further by changing the words to familiar tunes or inventing new words that fit – they don't have to make sense! In doing so you will discover some things about words and rhythm.

DID YOU KNOW?

Poets sometimes write new words to familiar tunes to create special effects. Wendy Cope (1945–), for instance, is fond of making satirical comment in this way. The familiar, uncomplicated, confident rhythms (and rhymes) seem to contrast with the human frailty to which the verses refer.

A Green Song
to sing at the bottle bank

One green bottle,
Drop it in the bank.
Ten green bottles
What a lot we drank.
Heaps of bottles
And yesterday's a blank
But we'll save the planet,
Tinkle, tinkle, clank!

We've got bottles –
Nice, percussive trash.
Bags of bottles
Cleaned us out of cash.
Empty bottles,
We love to hear them smash
And we'll save the planet,
Tinkle, tinkle, crash!

N
O
T
E
S

2 Rhyme and other noises

People love rhyme, children especially. Some believe that something that doesn't rhyme cannot possibly be poetry.

By no means all poetry rhymes but rhyme is one of the most obvious differences between verse and prose.

We seem to enjoy it because we look forward to the rhyme and gain some satisfaction when it arrives.

Comic verse often employs improbable or multiple rhymes. Consider this little poem by Ogden Nash (1902–71):

The Ant

The ant has made himself illustrious
Through constant industry industrious.
So what?
Would you be calm and placid
If you were full of formic acid?

DID YOU KNOW?

The composer and lyricist, Cole Porter was famous for his endlessly inventive rhyming. In his musical, *Anything Goes*, famous poets served the needs of rhyme in ways even they could not have suspected:

You're the top!
You're a hot tamale,
You're an angel, you, simply, too, too, too diveen,
You're a Botticelli,
You're Keats,
You're Shelley,
You're Ovaltine.

Sounding the same – a word about onomatopoeia

Many students set much store by the notion of onomatopoeia or the use of words whose sound seems to be the same as what they refer to such as 'snap, crackle, pop'.

Certainly, poets have always attempted onomatopoeic effects. For instance, Tennyson (that man again!) famously referred to 'The murmuring of innumerable bees'. However, it is unwise to take the effect too literally and it is better to think of it as sound symbolism rather than literal imitation. Otherwise, you can come to believe that almost any word or phrase imitates a sound.

Few words actually imitate a sound (and even these are open to dispute).

3　The line

In poetry the line has a particular importance:

- Poems are usually printed in a clear pattern of lines – each customarily beginning with a capital letter. (Many modern poets have deliberately broken with this tradition, however.)

- Lines form the framework for the poem's metre and line-endings usually mark a significant rhythmical point in the poem's development.

- Poems are often divided into groups of lines, often with an identical pattern, called verses or *stanzas*.

One important function of the line lies in the special way it affects the sense we take away from a poem.

This sentence makes perfect sense as it stands:

Among twenty snowy mountains the only moving thing was the eye of the blackbird.

But as originally written we are perhaps made more alert to the 'drama' of the scene and its three elements:

Among twenty snowy mountains,
The only moving thing
Was the eye of the blackbird.

(from **Thirteen Ways of Looking at a Blackbird**,
Wallace Stevens, 1879–1955)

Notice how you tend to pause slightly after 'thing' even though there is no strict need.

Line length and rhythmical effect are closely related

The way in which line divisions may organise a poem's sense may be called *line grammar* (which may or may not line up with the normal grammar).

DID YOU KNOW?
The effect of line grammar is very noticeable in free verse that does not have a strict formal rhythm. Compare the 'feel' of these two examples, one with short lines, one with long lines:

Two girls discover
the secret of life
in a sudden line of
poetry.
(from **The Secret** by Denise Levertov, 1923–)

Where are you now, Batman? Now that Aunt Heriot
reported Robin missing
And Superman's fallen asleep in the sixpenny childhood seats?
(from **Where are you now, Batman?**, Brian Patten, 1946–)

Line and Rhyme

The poetic line and the poem's *rhyme scheme* go hand in hand. In these lines from *In Memoriam* (1850), Alfred Lord Tennyson chooses an **abba** rhyme scheme (the pattern of rhymes):

Ring out the want, the care, the sin,	**a**
The faithless coldness of the times;	**b**
Ring out, ring out my mournful rhymes,	**b**
But ring the fuller minstrel in.	**a**

In other words, lines 1 and 4 rhyme (*sin / in*) and lines 2 and 3 rhyme (*times / rhymes*).

In general, there is no need concern yourself very much about rhyme schemes except perhaps when you meet a particularly striking pattern.

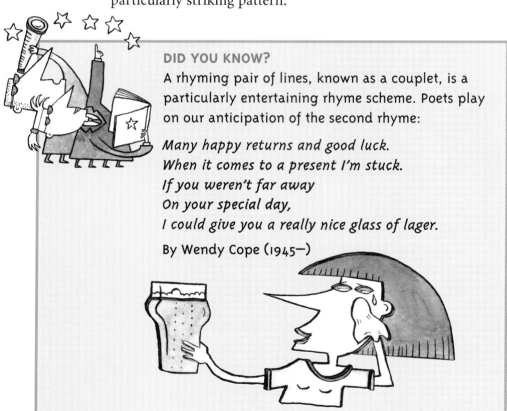

DID YOU KNOW?

A rhyming pair of lines, known as a couplet, is a particularly entertaining rhyme scheme. Poets play on our anticipation of the second rhyme:

Many happy returns and good luck.
When it comes to a present I'm stuck.
If you weren't far away
On your special day,
I could give you a really nice glass of lager.

By Wendy Cope (1945–)

DID YOU KNOW?

A limerick may seem like an 'easy' poem:

There was a young lady from Niger,
Who smiled as she rode on a tiger.
They returned from the ride
With the lady inside
And the smile on the face of the tiger.

But you might be surprised at the rules:

Five lines, mixing anapaests ▶ see p 56 and iambs
▶ see p 58, rhyming **aabba**.

KEY CONCEPTS

Poetry involves organising words into sound patterns ✳

What a poem conveys is a product of how it is written ✳

Rhythm is not something added to a poem nor does it have any particular meaning ✳

NOTES

HIGHER PERFORMANCE

In 1936, the documentary film director John Grierson, the composer, Benjamin Britten and the poet W.H. Auden collaborated to make a film for The General Post Office film unit, depicting the overnight mail train steaming its way to Scotland. It was called *Night Mail*. Auden's poem and Britten's music used a range of techniques to match the movements of the steam train. How many techniques and devices can you uncover in this section of Auden's poem?

I

This is the Night Mail crossing the Border,
Bringing the cheque and the postal order,

Letters for the rich, letters for the poor,
The shop at the corner, the girl next door.

Pulling up Beattock, a steady climb:
The gradient's against her, but she's on time.

Past cotton-grass and moorland boulder,
Shovelling white steam over her shoulder,

Snorting noisily, she passes
Silent miles of wind-bent grasses.

Birds turn their heads as she approaches,
Stare from bushes at her blank-faced coaches.

Sheep-dogs cannot turn her course;
They slumber on with paws across.

In the farm she passes no one wakes,
But a jug in a bedroom gently shakes.

II

Dawn freshens. Her climb is done.
Down towards Glasgow she descends,
Towards the steam tugs yelping down a glade of cranes,
Towards the fields of apparatus, the furnaces
Set on the dark plain like gigantic chessmen.
All Scotland waits for her:
In dark glens, beside pale-green lochs,
Men long for news.

Quiz

1. Indicate the stresses in the following names:
a David   b Elizabeth   c Abigail   d Michelle?

2. From the extract by Milton ▶ see p 57
pick out the example of three
stressed syllables in a row.

3. What rhythm, iambic (ti-**tum**)
or trochaic (**tum**-ti), has this
famous line?
I wandered lonely as a cloud

4. In *The Loving Dexterity* ▶ see p 59 the words and
phrases, 'flower', 'fallen', 'saw it', 'petal', 'deftly',
'placed it' are all miniature examples of what rhythm?

5. What term is used here to refer to the
effect line divisions in poetry have
on meaning?

6. Look at the two lines from the poem
by Brian Patten ▶ see p 65. Where
are the sixpenny childhood seats?

7. Anticlimax is a descent from the
sublime to the ridiculous. What
word produces an anticlimax in
the extract from Cole Porter's
Anything Goes ▶ see p 63?

Answers

1 a) **David** b) **Elizabeth**
   c) **Abigail** d) Michelle
2 *dark, dark, dark*
3 Iambic
4 Trochaic
5 Line grammar
6 In a cinema
7 Ovaltine

PUTTING IT ALL TOGETHER
– HOW TO APPROACH A POEM

Strategies
Meaning
Writing about it

Face to face with a poem

What does one do when faced with the task of writing about a poem? The not very helpful answer is 'It depends on the poem'.

Every poem makes its own individual demands on the reader and the mix of qualities is never quite the same.

There are no universal rules for analysing a poem but there are a number of strategies that it is possible to adopt:

- First, **form a general impression of the poem** and gather ideas about different aspects of the writing. DO NOT treat it as prose written in a strange and inconvenient way.

- Look at the poem and say it over to yourself. Don't be over-concerned about the exact sense but **try to judge the mood and general 'feel' and nature of the text**. What do you think is the centre of interest in the poem? Do any features catch your attention – an unusual turn of phrase, a play on words, a striking rhythm, an intriguing idea...?

- If you think you cannot understand the poem at all, **try to work out exactly where your understanding breaks down** – you may be able to skip that difficult bit and return to it later.

- Your task is then to **build on your impressions and draw them into a sensible whole**, not so easy but never impossible.

- Remember what we have said about meaning and theme. **What is the purpose of the poem?** Is the poet exploring a theme, thinking about an aspect of experience, exploring a private world, experimenting with words, telling a story, singing a song or any combination of such aims?

DID YOU KNOW?

Alliteration refers to the repetition of consonants with the same **sound**.

Assonance refers to the repetition of the same vowel **sounds**.

Do not confuse letters with the sound they represent. Cement and concrete do not alliterate nor is there any assonance.

- **Consider the way the poem is written**, the imagery, the rhythms, rhymes and verbal effects, such as alliteration and assonance. But remember there is little profit in simply spotting technical features. You will gain far more credit and achieve a greater understanding if you can show how the poet's techniques relate to the meaning of the poem.

N
O
T
E
S

Talking about some poems

Oddly enough, some of the hardest poems to handle are very short poems. This is because they are often no more than snapshots, a moment of reflection, a chance observation. Take, for instance, this little poem by Richard Kenney (1948–):

Plume
In the orchard,
puffs, plumes,
odd gusts –
when suddenly
the trees toss up
their blooms at once:
white petals
chimney up
and braid together
in the sky
like sweet smoke
from the same flame –
so beautiful!
And still, a shame.

What did you notice?

- The most obvious feature of the poem is that it is a short poem with very short lines. What would you might expect from such a short poem (a mere 41 words in all)? You expect concentration and focus, which is exactly what we get.

- The poem concerns itself with a fleeting observation of wind catching the spring blossom from trees in an orchard and sweeping it up into the sky. It is the sort of incident that would normally pass without comment. There is nothing extraordinary about these circumstances, except that the poet pauses to observe and like a skilled photographer composes the scene in his verbal lens.

- On closer examination, it turns out that most of the poem is made up of a single sentence.

- What is striking, however, is the line grammar ▶ see p 65 which divides that sentence into little parcels of sense, each with a two-stress pulse.

- The effect is most easily demonstrated if we look at the sentence written out in prose:

  In the orchard, puffs, plumes, odd gusts – when suddenly the trees toss up their blooms at once: white petals chimney up and braid together in the sky like sweet smoke from the same flame – so beautiful!

  We are still presented with gentle description, but the sense of movement is much less well defined. It fails to trace the delicate steps with which the blossom is seen to rise. Whereas, in the poem, we follow each moment of the poet's perception, in the prose version one detail merges into the next. (Say both versions over to yourself.)

- We also lose something of the sense of concentration on each little detail. Look, for instance, at the line 'chimney up'. The poet has a noun in a verbal sense, which throws our attention on to the shape and movement of the petals at that particular point. Notice, too, how delicately the poet sustains the comparison between the blossom and smoke.

What does the poem mean?

- You could argue that the poet confronts us with the paradox (a statement that seems contradictory) that there is beauty in destruction. If, however, you pay attention to the tone, or mood, of the last line, as well as its sense, you will see that Richard Kenney is making no claims to be profound. A passing moment leads to a passing thought about the fragile beauty of the natural world.

At Grass

The eye can hardly pick them out
From the cold shade they shelter in,
Till wind distresses tail and mane;
Then one crops grass, and moves about
– The other seeming to look on –
And stands anonymous again.

Yet fifteen years ago, perhaps
Two dozen distances sufficed
To fable them: faint afternoons
Of Cups and Stakes and Handicaps,
Whereby their names were artificed
To inlay faded, classic Junes –

Silks at the start: against the sky
Numbers and parasols: outside,
Squadrons of empty cars, and heat,
And littered grass: then the long cry
Hanging unhushed till it subside
To stop-press columns on the street.

Do memories plague their cars like flies?
They shake their heads. Dusk brims the shadows.
Summer by summer all stole away,
The starting-gates, the crowds and cries –
All but the unmolesting meadows.
Almanacked, their names live; they

Have slipped their names, and stand at ease,
Or gallop for what must be joy,
And not a fieldglass sees them home,
Or curious stop-watch prophesies:
Only the groom, and the groom's boy
With bridles in the evening come.

(Philip Larkin, 1922–85)

What did you notice?

- Like *Plume, At Grass* appears to capture a chance observation. There seems nothing remarkable about the poem's appearance or layout and reading for the basic sense is quite straightforward – which is usually a sign that we have to dig a little deeper!

- The 'plot' of the poem is quite simple. The narrator sees two horses in the distance, grazing quietly. The middle three stanzas are a flashback to the days when they were champion racehorses, whilst the final stanza returns to the present.

- The poem's bright centre, made up of compact and vivid phrases, captures the atmosphere of race day. In a single stanza, Larkin has compressed a kaleidoscope of sound and sense from the start of the race ('silks') to the race results in the evening papers ('the stop-press columns on the street').

- That excitement is contrasted with the quieter mood of the horses at grass. The fourth stanza beautifully captures the receding images of the racecourse ('the starting gates, the crowds and cries') mingling with a return to the present.

What is the poem really about?

- This is a finely descriptive poem about horses, comparing their present and past. Nevertheless, it takes only a small leap of the imagination to appreciate that the poet's concern is also the fleeting nature of fame and popularity. How many once-famous stars are soon forgotten by the society that adored them?

- However, Larkin is not judgemental. He only watches and wonders. He does not assume that the loss of fame necessarily leads to frustration and unhappiness; the horses after all 'gallop for what must be joy'.

The Lament of the Banana Man

Gal, I'm tellin you, I'm tired fo true,
Tired of Englan, tired o you.
But I can't go back to Jamaica now ...

I'm here in Englan, I'm drawin pay,
I go to de underground every day –
Eight hours is all, half-hour fo lunch,
M' uniform's free, an m'ticket punch –
Punchin tickets not hard to do,
When I'm tired o punchin, I let dem through.

I get a paid holiday once a year.
Ol age an sickness can't touch me here.
I have a room of m'own, an a iron bed,
Dunlopillo under m'head,
A Morphy-Richards to warm de air,
A formica table, an easy chair.
I have summer clothes, an winter clothes,
An paper kerchiefs to blow m'nose.

My yoke is easy, my burden is light,
I know a place I can go to, any night.
Dis place Englan! I'm not complainin,
If it col', it col', if it rainin, it rainin.
I don't mind if it's mostly night,
Dere's always inside, or de sodium light.
I don't mind white people starin at me,
Dey don' want me here? Don't is deir country?
You won' catch me bawlin any homesick tears,
If I don' see Jamaica for a t'ousan years!

... Gal, I'm tellin you, I'm tired fo true,
Tired of Englan, tired o you,
I can't go back to Jamaica now –
But I'd want to die there, anyhow.

(Evan Jones, 1927–)

What did you notice?

- 'Banana Man' refers to thousands of West Indians brought to the UK in the 1950s to alleviate a shortage of workers. The phrase has derogatory connotations.

- The most obvious feature of the poem is the adoption of some West Indian speech forms ('tellin', 'fo', 'Englan', 'col'...).

- The rhythm is assertive and the verse has an insistent beat. A blend of colloquial word-forms and a rhythmical framework establish an authentic Caribbean 'voice'.

- The line structure is quite formal: the end of each line is marked by a clear stress, a firm rhyme and a distinct pause in sense. Each line itself falls into two parts: *I'm here in 'Englan / I'm drawin pay.* This break in the body of a line is known as a caesura and is common in poetry.

- The poem is full of alliterative patterns (the repetitive 't' in the first stanza, for instance) and assonance (Jamaica-pay-day-eight-paid-holiday-complainin-rainin).

- All these features set the poem within a distinctive musical and oral tradition.

- The man says that he is fed up with England but generally cannot complain. If we examine this, however, we discover a clear irony. His job is undemanding but monotonous and dreary; he has a 'room' but few possessions; he is depressed by the gloom but takes comfort in artificial light; he endures 'white people starin' but claims he is used to it. The irony is that his comforts are no more than a prison; as a West Indian in England his only sense of belonging is through owning a few meagre products.

- His frustration is in the outer stanzas. His life and marriage are in crisis. He is 'tired' but helpless to do anything about it. The most he can hope is to die in Jamaica.

- The message is a poignant and bitter but is told with warmth and individuality. A vein of humour creates a positive effect.

N
O
T
E
S

Comparing and contrasting poems

You will need to know how to compare and contrast poems by the same author or by different authors.

Remember that comparing texts includes finding differences as well as similarities.

You may compare

- The subject-matter of the poem
- The mood and tone of each poem
- The way they are written
- The purpose of the author or authors
- The 'message' of each piece
- The effects on the reader

but not necessarily all those features or in that order.
It is possible to compare poems continuously, referring back and forth from one poem to another, or to treat each poem individually.

KEY CONCEPTS

✳ You need to approach each poem with an open mind

✳ You should be prepared to probe each poem considering a range of possible factors

✳ In a given poem, some features may be much more important than others

✳ You should try to see how the meaning of a poem and how it is written are related

N
O
T
E
S

SOME DON'TS AND DOS

Don't use the expression 'The poet says ...' (at least use it with extreme care). As you should have learned poets rarely simply say!

Do use expressions (where appropriate) like 'The poet suggests / conveys / stresses / evokes / hints / dramatises / illustrates...' But not all at once!

Don't say things like 'You can tell what the poet means by the way she uses language'. What else can a poet use but language?

Do say things like 'the poet conveys his anger by his stress on the word ****'

Don't summarise or tell the story of a poem for the sake of it. The reader / examiner will have read the poem already.

Do illustrate each comment you make with a reference to the text. This need not always be a direct quotation.

Don't write out quotations at length. All that proves is that you can copy.

Do try to quote the exact word or phrase that proves your point. Long quotations are too imprecise.

Do get to a good start by making a firm point in your first sentence, especially in examination conditions when you have no time for introductions.

Don't use technical terms if you don't really understand them.

Do use technical terms if you do understand them!

Don't repeat the question or task as the beginning of your answer and don't waste a paragraph grandly announcing what you are about to write about.

HIGHER PERFORMANCE

You can probably find a poem on almost any subject you care to name – maybe not differential gears – but who knows? However, one of the most fascinating aspects of poetry is the enormous variety of ways poets find of looking at the same subject.

Lat take a cat and fostre hym wel with milk
And tendre flessch and make his couche of silk,
And lat hym seen a mouse go by the wal,
Anon he weyvith milk and flessch and al,
And every deyntee that is in that hous,
Suich appetit he hath to ete a mous.

(from **The Manciple's Tale**, Geoffrey Chaucer, 1343?–1400)

Cat, nine days old, knit out of soot,
Fragile and scrawny, squirms in the cupped palm;
Mewls, pukes, and gestures with four needy paws:
Milk; sleep; warmth; that brusque abrasive tongue
Which scours, explores the rank damp-clinging fur
Already cat, not pussy

(from **Cat**, William Dunlop)

Explore how the poets treat their subjects and compare the two poems. Are there any similarities in the poets' views. What are the differences?

Quiz

1. What is being described in *Plume* see p 72?

2. In *At Grass* see p 74 what is significant about the horses being anonymous?

3. To what do 'Cups and Stakes and Handicaps' refer?

4. To what does the word 'silks' refer?

5. What does the term 'almanacked' suggest?

6. What does the 'Banana Man' see p 76 do for a living?

7. What lines suggest the presence of the 'Banana Man' is resented in his adopted country?

Answers

1 The blossom of fruit trees being carried in the wind

2 They are no longer in the public eye/ they no longer carry their official racing names.

3 The races in which the horses competed

4 The jockeys' official kit

5 The results of the horses' races have been officially recorded.

6 Collects tickets on the underground

7 *I don't mind white people starin at me, / Dey don' want me here?*

THE RISE OF POETRY

A history of poetry in English
Some poems from different times

Beginnings

The earliest English poetry we know about appeared in
manuscripts dating from about 1000AD. It was originally
intended to be chanted, or declaimed, and was probably
performed from memory long before it was ever written down.
  It looked like this:

> MÆg ic be me sylfum   soðgied wrecan,
> siþas secgan,   hu ic geswincdagum
> earfoðhwile   oft þrowade,
> bitre breostceare   gebiden hæbbe,
> gecunnad in ceole   cearselda fela,
> atol yþa gewealc,   þær mec oft bigeat
> nearo nihtwaco   æt nacan stefnan,
> þonne he be clifum cnossað.   Calde geþrungen

This is the opening of *The Seafarer* in which the narrator
announces that he is going to tell of his travels and the
hardships he endured. It is written in Old English. It looks very
strange but if it were read aloud properly, you would easily
appreciate the strong beat and vivid alliteration – even if you
did not understand a word.

About 300 years later English poetry looked rather more familiar:

Blow, northerne wynd,
sent thou me my suetyng !
Blow, northerne wynd,
Blou! blou! blou!

This is one of a group of lyric poems known as *The Harley Lyrics* (1314–25) and is an example of Middle English verse.

Shortly after the appearance of *The Harley Lyrics*, the first undisputed great name in English poetry was born. He was Geoffrey Chaucer (1343?–1400). His most famous work is *The Canterbury Tales.* The 'Tales' are told by a group of pilgrims on their journey to Canterbury. They are a very mixed crew and the stories they tell reflect everything from the elegant sophistication of the Knight to the earthy bawdy (sauciness) of the Miller. *The General Prologue to The Canterbury Tales* is particularly notable for its sharp observation and witty suggestiveness.

Sixteenth to seventeenth century

This period is sometimes referred to as the English Renaissance and it was marked by a particularly rich flowering of all the arts. The two most prominent figures in the first part of this period were Edmund Spenser (1552?–99) and Sir Philip Sidney (1554–86). Spenser's great (in all senses of the word) poem, *The Faerie Queene* proved that it was possible to write a poetic masterpiece in English.

Late seventeenth to eighteenth century

The most notable poet of the seventeenth century was John Milton (1608–74) see p 58. His great poem *Paradise Lost* (1667) told of the events from Satan's rebellion in Heaven to Adam and Eve's expulsion from the Garden of Eden.

From, 1660, thought and literature took a new turn – what has come to be known as The Age of Reason. Philosophy flourished and the new rational thinking was reflected in poetry as an emphasis on elegance, balance and order.

The outstanding figure of the late seventeenth century was John Dryden (1631–1700) who did much to establish the new public voice for poetry. His *Alexander's Feast* and *A Song for St. Cecilia's Day* are perhaps best known in their musical settings by George Frederick Handel.

The first half of the eighteenth century was dominated by the work of Alexander Pope (1688–1744) see p 58. His writing combines poise and fluency with an acute alertness to every aspect of human frailty.

In the late 1700s there was an increasing demand for social and political change. This manifested itself in the American Declaration of Independence in 1776 and in the French Revolution of 1789.

Personal freedom was of the utmost importance, and the ultimate expression of personal freedom was the imagination. Romanticism was born.

The Romantic Age

This revolutionary fervour is nowhere more in evidence than in the poetry of William Blake (1757–1827) ● see p 43, who published his *Songs of Innocence* in 1789, followed by the *Songs of Experience* in 1794.

In 1798, *Lyrical Ballads* by William Wordsworth (1770–1850) and Samuel Taylor Coleridge (1772–1834) burst on the scene. Although Wordsworth set great store by their use of natural language, it is the way they began to explore and exploit the inner workings of the mind that strikes us as most original today. Wordsworth's *Lines composed a few miles above Tintern Abbey* is perhaps the first great poem to explore the nature and power of memory. Coleridge's *The Rime of the Ancient Mariner* explored the darker aspects of our imagination.

DID YOU KNOW?

The Rime of the Ancient Mariner is a tale of a voyage into a world of living nightmare. Along with some popular novels of the day it forms the beginning of a tradition that leads to today's horror movies.

Within a few years, John Keats (1795–1821) ● see pp 14–15 created a new, rich poetic language in which thought and feeling combine in a uniquely intense way.

Other leading figures in the English romantic movement included Lord George Byron (1788–1824) and Percy Bysshe Shelley (1792–1822).

All the romantic poets found inspiration in Nature, whether real or imagined.

N
O
T
E
S

The Victorian Age

The leading poets of Victorian England were Robert Browning (1812–89) see pp 34–35, 48 and Alfred Lord Tennyson (1809–92) see p 29. Tennyson had a remarkable ear for the sound of words.

Gerard Manley Hopkins (1844–89) see p 42, whose work was virtually unknown until 1918, also experimented with bold rhythms.

During the nineteenth century the increasingly industrialised environment was felt by many to be impersonal, harsh and soulless. Thomas Hardy (1840–1928) and Alfred Edward (always known as A.E.) Housman (1859–1936) in his *A Shropshire Lad* (1896) turned back to the English countryside for consolation. They did not always find the comfort they sought but they helped to establish a particular brand of poignant nostalgia, sometimes referred to as 'English pastoral'.

The nineteenth century also saw the emergence of American poets, including Henry Wadsworth Longfellow (1807–82), Edgar Allan Poe (1809–49), Walt Whitman (1819–92) and Emily Dickinson (1830–86) see p 18.

In many ways, the American poets had a liberating influence on the future of poetry.

Emily Dickinson, virtually none of whose work was published in her lifetime, was at first regarded as a rather quaint eccentric. Now her work is appreciated for its startling originality and modernity. The candour and freedom of Whitman's poetry was regarded as a break with European stuffiness.

The twentieth century

Poetry in the twentieth century has been remarkably rich and diverse. In general, there has been a trend away from the larger forms and grand statements towards shorter poems that hold aspects of life in close focus.

Poets have also tended to adopt a flexible, conversational tone, whilst at the same time being ready to experiment with a variety of poetic forms, sometimes within the same poem.

Thomas Stearns (abbreviated to T.S.) Eliot (1888–1965) was a key figure in establishing the modern poetic 'voice'. His concentrated and complex poetic cycle, *The Waste Land* (1922), confronted what he saw as the futility and emptiness of modern life. It made a profound impression at a time when the arts seemed to be at war with the forces of science and technology.

HIGHER PERFORMANCE

This extract from *The Waste Land* defies traditional metrical analysis and yet is highly organised. Notice how Eliot mimics the tones of ragtime (a kind of music) and bunches snippets of dialogue into rhythmical clusters:

O O O O that Shakespeherian Rag –
It's so elegant
So intelligent
'What shall I do now? What shall I do?'
'I shall rush out as I am, and walk the street
'With my hair down, so. What shall we do tomorrow?

(from **The Waste Land** – II A Game of Chess)

Equally, if not more, influential was the Irish poet, William Butler Yeats (1865–1939) who used ordinary speech forms to create intense lyrical poetry:

The Arrow

I thought of your beauty, and this arrow,
Made out of a wild thought, is in my marrow.
There's no man may look upon her, no man,
As when newly grown to be a woman,
Tall and noble but with face and bosom
Delicate in colour as apple blossom.
This beauty's kinder, yet for a reason
I could weep that the old is out of season.

(W.B. Yeats, 1904)

Yeats was deeply admired by W.H. Auden (1907–73). His tribute to Yeats has the weight and tone of the traditional elegy (a poem that laments someone's death), but is thoroughly modern in spirit:

He disappeared in the dead of winter:
The brooks were frozen, the airports almost deserted,
And snow disfigured the public statues;
The mercury sank in the mouth of the dying day.
What instruments we have agree
The day of his death was a dark cold day.

(from **In Memory of W.B. Yeats**)

A similar control of movement and stress within more or less natural speech patterns is a common feature of modern poetry:

He sipped at a weak hock and selzer
As he gazed at the London skies

(from **The Arrest of Oscar Wilde at the Cadogan Hotel**, John Betjeman, 1906–84)

This house has been far out at sea all night,
The woods crashing through darkness, ...

(from **Wind** by Ted Hughes, 1930–98)

But don't think that today's poets have forgotten traditional rhyme and rhythm!

When the words have gone away
there is nothing left to say.

(from **Alphabet for Auden** by Carol Ann Duffy, 1955–)

An interesting feature of twentieth-century poetry has been its readiness to confront social and political issues. Wilfred Owen (1893–1918), Siegfried Sassoon (1886–1967) ⬤ see p 16, 27 and others who had experienced the horrors of the First World War expressed their outrage. Poets have fought for justice, the environment, the rights of women and social and ethnic minorities.

DID YOU KNOW?

On 24 February, 1999, Benjamin Zephaniah appeared on Channel Four news to perform his poem on the report of the inquiry into the death of the black teenager, Stephen Lawrence.

Aliens among us

1. As well as conveying meaning, why do poets use the words they do?
2. What is an allusion?
3. Who said, 'when the seagulls follow the trawler it is because they think sardines will be thrown into the sea'?
4. Why does the prisoner in *Jailbird* have 'dun plumage?'
5. What is a metaphor?
6. Which famous film star was called Marion Morrison?
7. Why do poets use imagery rather than factual language?
8. How do poets make us think about their poems?
9. Why do manufacturers use poetic names to describe their products?
10. Why do manufacturers not use German-sounding names for their products?

Answers

1. To stir feelings and emotions.
2. An unexplained reference.
3. Eric Cantona.
4. It is the colour of his drab prison uniform.
5. It is a comparison which is made without writing 'like' or 'as'.
6. John Wayne.
7. Imagery makes a greater impression on the reader.
8. They use imagery, word play, allusion...
9. Because poetry touches the emotions, the manufacturers know that hearts rather than heads often buy products.
10. German is guttural and uses lots of consonants. It is not a particularly romantic-sounding language!

Did you get it?

Different sorts of poetry

1. Poetry is not always dreamy. What else can it convey?
2. What sort of insect did Peter Kane Dufault write about in 1978?
3. How is poetry intended to be performed?
4. What is an Epic?
5. Who wrote the Caribbean Epic, *Omeros* (1981)
6. What has lyric poetry traditionally been associated with?
7. How many syllables does a haiku have?
8. What does blank verse most closely resemble?
9. What is free verse?
10. What is satirical poetry often written in?

Answers

1. Cynicism, shock, fun, drama, humour ...
2. A mud dauber wasp!
3. By the human voice.
4. A long narrative poem dealing with a serious subject.
5. Derek Walcott.
6. Music and love.
7. Seventeen.
8. Natural English speech.
9. Poetry that is not tied to any specified verse form.
10. Rhyming couplets.

Meaning in Poetry

1. How does poetry differ from newspaper and book prose?
2. What is narrative poetry?
3. Apart from building up a picture, why do poets use description?
4. Why do we have to be careful with the 'Deceptive I' in poetry?
5. What happened to the poet John Clare and where did he spend the last years of his life?
6. Which account of The Charge of the Heavy Brigade do you find most interesting and why?
7. About which war did Siegfried Sassoon write poetry?
8. In Herbert Read's *The Scene of War: the Happy Warrior* can we tell which World War he is writing about?
9. How do poets try and make sense of the world?
10. What did John Clare's friends do to him, according to his poem *I am*?

Answers

1. It aims to convey more meaning than the literal.
2. Poetry that tells a story or recounts events.
3. Description may have a deeper significance for the reader than mere visual colour.
4. The 'I' may not necessarily be the one who is speaking.
5. He became mentally ill and spent his last few years in a lunatic asylum.
6. ▶ see p 29
7. The First World War.
8. Not really – The scene could come from either the First or Second World War. The use of the derogatory word 'Boche', meaning 'German' was used in both World Wars.
9. They never take anything at face value.
10. They forsook him.

Did you get it?

Weird and wonderful words

1. In which book does Jabberwocky appear?
2. What is the effect of the first two stanzas of Gerard Manley Hopkins's *Inversnaid*?
3. What is connotation?
4. In The Tyger, which animal is associated with Jesus Christ?
5. What mood is Vermon Scannell conveying in *View From a Deckchair*?
6. Imagery includes which figures of speech?
7. Who are 'Wasps in a bottle, frogs in a sieve'?
8. What is the theme of D.T. Enwright's poem *Blue Umbrellas*?
9. Whose glove is a 'snowy farm with five tenements'?
10. What is a vital ingredient of poetry?

Answers

1. *Through The Looking Glass* by Lewis Carroll.
2. It gives the feeling of a torrent of water gushing down.
3. Secondary meaning, overtone and association. What words suggest rather than mean literally
4. The Lamb.
5. A contented and peaceful mood.
6. Metaphor and simile
7. The persecuted Jews in Robert Browning's poem *Holy-Cross Day*
8. A child's imagination.
9. Ellinda's.
10. Connotation.

Rhythm and Rhyme

1. What is rhythm?
2. What is a metre?
3. Which rhythm has the ti-tum stress?
4. Which rhythm is rare?
5. Which rhythm has 'pattering feet'?
6. What is onomatopoeia?
7. What is a limerick?
8. Who wants to save the planet at the bottle bank?
9. Many modern West Indian poets build on which tradition?
10. How many metrical feet does free verse have?

Answers

1. Alternation of stressed and unstressed syllables.
2. A particular pattern or number of stresses in a line of poetry.
3. Iambic.
4. Anapaest.
5. Dactyl.
6. Words or phrases that sound similar to what they are referring to.
7. Five lines, mixing anapaests and iambs, rhyming **ababa**
8. Wendy Cope.
9. Caribbean Folk Tradition.
10. Any number – free verse does not obey traditional rules.

Putting it all together

1. What is the first thing that you should do when you are faced with a poem?
2. Then what should you look at?
3. What is alliteration?
4. What is assonance?
5. What is Richard Kenney's *Plume* about?
6. How does Philip Larkin's poem *At Grass* convey the fleeting nature of fame and popularity?
7. How does the *Banana Man* feel about living in England?
8. What should you not do with quotations?
9. What should you do with quotations?
10. What do Geoffrey Chaucer and William Dunlop have in common?

Answers

1. Read it through, perhaps aloud, and gain a general impression of it.
2. Mood, theme, purpose, rhythm and rhyme, to create a greater understanding.
3. Repetition of consonants with the same sound.
4. Repetition of vowels with the same sound.
5. ❍ see pp 72–73
6. ❍ see pp 74–75
7. ❍ see pp 76–77
8. Merely copy them out.
9. Quote the exact word or phrase that proves your point.
10. They both wrote poems based on observations of cats.

Index